Contents

der Würfel (the dice) - 2

das Eis (ice creams) - 3

die Familie (family) - 4

die Farben (colours) - 5

das Federmäppchen (the pencil case) - - - - - - - - - - - 6

das Gemüse (the vegetables) - - - - - - - - - - - - - - - 8

die Getränke (the drinks) - - - - - - - - - - - - - - - - 10

das Haus (the house) - - - - - - - - - - - - - - - - - - - 12

die Möbel (the furniture) - - - - - - - - - - - - - - - - 14

der Nachtisch (the dessert) - - - - - - - - - - - - - - - 16

das Obst (the fruit) - 18

die Stadt (the town / city) - - - - - - - - - - - - - - - - 20

die Tiere (the animals) - - - - - - - - - - - - - - - - - - 22

die Transportmittel (the transport) - - - - - - - - - - - 24

das Wetter (the weather) - - - - - - - - - - - - - - - - 26

der Zoo (the zoo) - 27

Der Würfel (the dice)

To make the dice:

Photocopy or trace the dice.

With an adult cut out the dice.

Fold down the sections marked x.

Fold the lines in between the dice faces.

Fold the dice together, and glue the sections marked x.

drei

sechs

fünf

vier

zwei

eins

To play the number game:

Role the dice, and say in German the number you get.

The next player roles the dice, and says the number they get.

Whoever gets the biggest number in each round gets a point, and if two players get the same number they both get a point.

The winner is the first person to get five points.

Das Eis (the ice creams)

The idea of this game is to be the first to draw an ice cream sundae with 6 different flavours. For this game you will need a dice, and each player will need a piece of paper and a pencil. Before you start the game draw just the dish for your ice cream sundae at the bottom of your page.

Take turns to roll the dice, and say the German word for the corresponding ice cream flavour. If you haven't got the ice cream flavour yet for the dice you have thrown draw a ball of ice cream in your sundae dish and label the flavour in German. Who will be the first to get 6 different ice cream flavours?

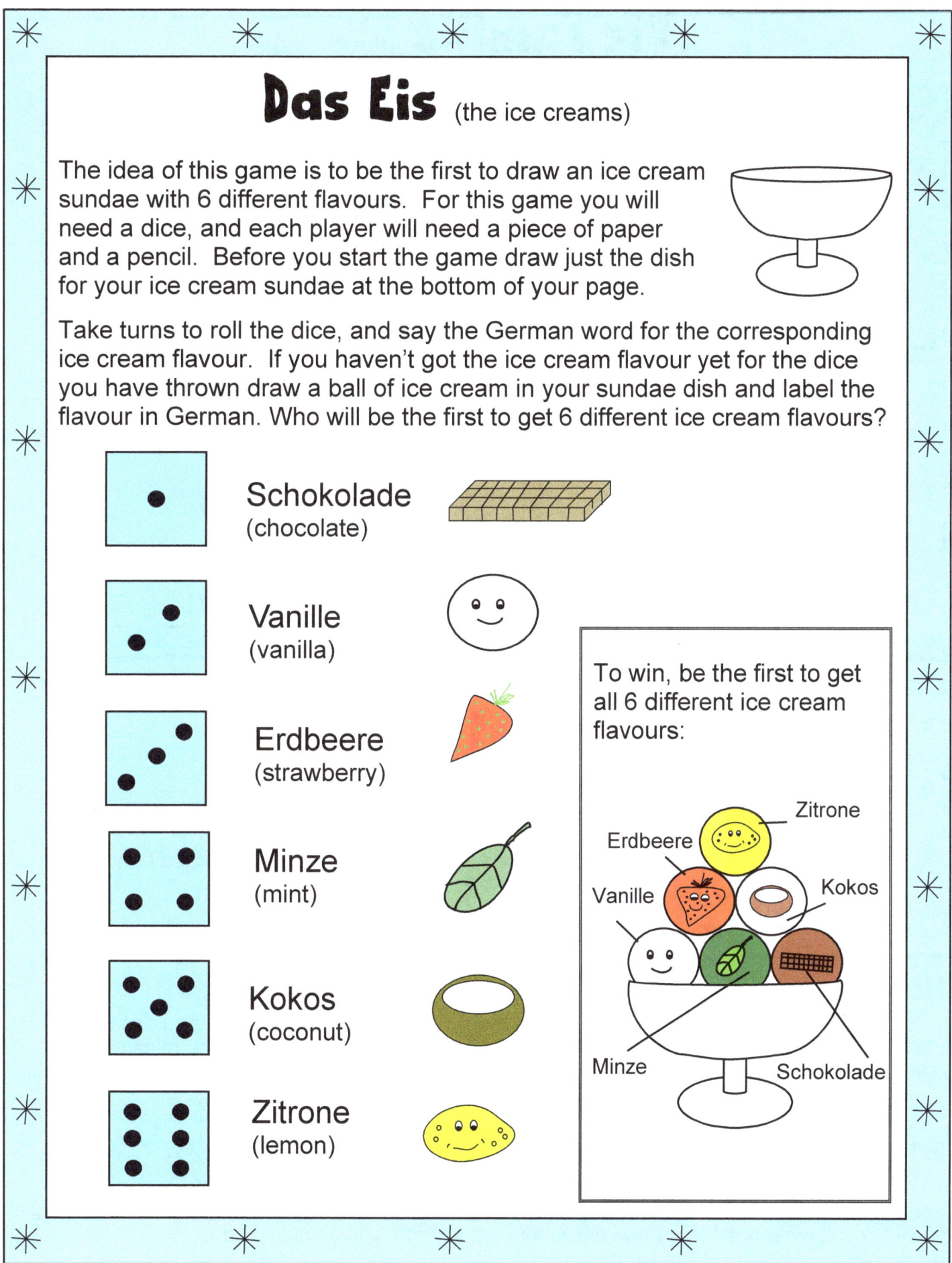

- ⚀ Schokolade (chocolate)
- ⚁ Vanille (vanilla)
- ⚂ Erdbeere (strawberry)
- ⚃ Minze (mint)
- ⚄ Kokos (coconut)
- ⚅ Zitrone (lemon)

To win, be the first to get all 6 different ice cream flavours:

Die Familie (the family)

How to play

To play the happy families card game in two teams, you will need to photocopy this page twice. (Or photocopy this page by the number of players if you each want to collect a set of cards)
With an adult cut out the 6 cards per page. (Or make your own cards by copying the pictures and German words)

The idea of this game is to be the first to get the six different cards:

der Opa, die Oma, der Vater, die Mutter, der Bruder, die Schwester

To play: Place the cards face down. Take turns to turn over ONE card. Say the word in German. Keep the card if you haven't yet got that card. If you have the card, place the card in a pile. This pile of cards can be arranged face down once there are no more cards to turn over.

Who will be the first to get all 6 cards?

Die Farben (colours)

Number of players: 2   Each player will need 5 counters
(The counters can be cubes, rubbers, or home made on pieces of paper.)

Take turns to place one of your counters on the board as you say the colour you are choosing in German.

To win you need to get three counters in a row either vertically, horizontally or diagonally.

Das Federmäppchen (the pencil case)

Imagine you are buying a new pencil case and some things to put in it. To win, be the first person to get the following six items:

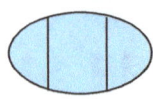 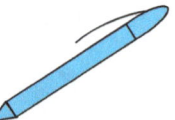

der Radiergummi (the rubber)   **der Bleistift** (the pencil)   **der Kugelschreiber** (the pen)

 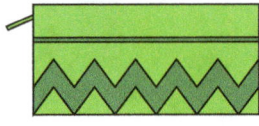

der Spitzer (the pencil sharpener)   **das Lineal** (the ruler)   **das Federmäppchen** (the pencil case)

To play:

Place your counter on Start. Roll the dice and move your counter that number of spaces. Count the number of spaces in German.

1	2	3	4	5	6
eins	zwei	drei	vier	fünf	sechs

If you arrive at one of the items, say the German word for the item pictured, and if you haven't got it yet, draw the item and write the word in German. Take turns to roll the dice.

If you arrive at a **X** you have to lose an item. You can choose which item you lose. Who will be the first to get all six items?

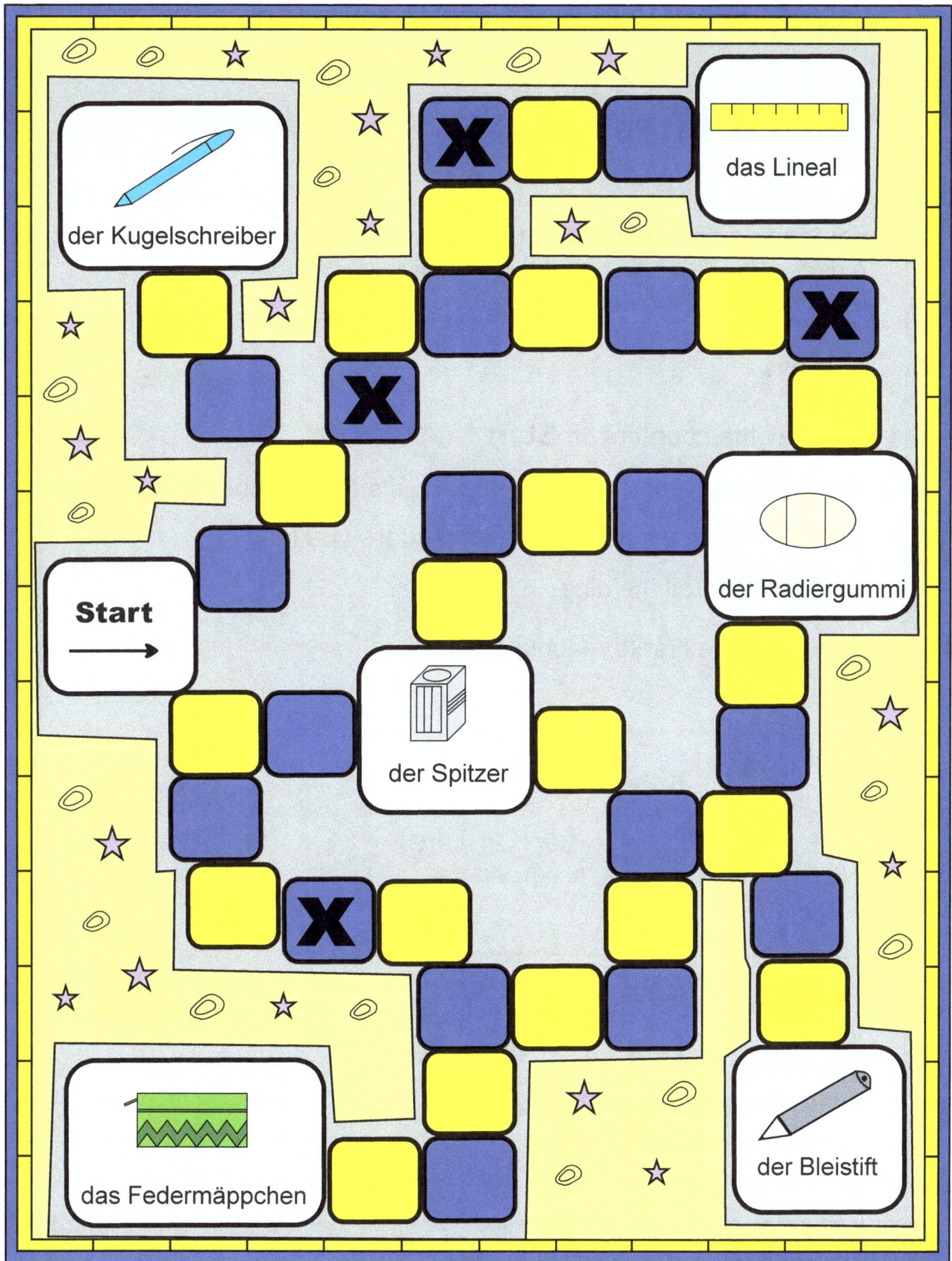

Das Gemüse (the vegetables)

For the vegetables game you will need:
A **dice** (You can use a normal dice or make the dice on page 2.)
A **counter for each player** (You can use cubes, rubbers or make your own)

To play:

Place all the counters on **Start**.

The first player rolls the dice, and counts that number of spaces.

Say in German what is in the final square you land on.

Take turns to roll the dice.

To win, be the first to reach **Ziel**.

die Karotte
(the carrot)

die Kartoffel
(the potato)

die Zwiebel
(the onion)

die Bohnen
(the beans)

die Erbsen
(the peas)

die Pilze
(the mushrooms)

Die Getränke (the drinks)

For the snakes & ladders game you will need:
A **dice** (You can use a normal dice or make the dice on page 2.)
A **counter for each player** (You can use cubes, rubbers or make your own.)

To play:

Place all the counters on **Start**.

The first player rolls the dice, and counts that number of spaces.

If there is a ladder in the final square, go up it.

If there is a snake in the final square, go down it.

Say in German what is in the final square you land on.

Take turns to roll the dice. To win, be the first to reach **Ziel**.

die Limonade (lemonade)   **die Cola** (coca-cola)   **das Wasser** (water)

der Orangensaft (orange juice)   **der Kaffee** (coffee)   **der Tee** (tea)

Das Haus (the house)

For the house game you will need:
A **dice** (You can use a normal dice or make the dice on page 2.)
A **counter for each player** (You can use cubes, rubbers or make your own)

To play:

Place all the counters on **Start**.

The first player rolls the dice, and counts that number of spaces.

Say in German what is in the final square you land on.

Take turns to roll the dice. To win, be the first to reach **Ziel**.

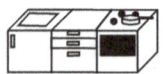  

die Küche (the kitchen)   **das Wohnzimmer** (the living room)   **das Esszimmer** (the dining room)

die Garage (the garage)   **die Tür** (the door)   **das Fenster** (the window)

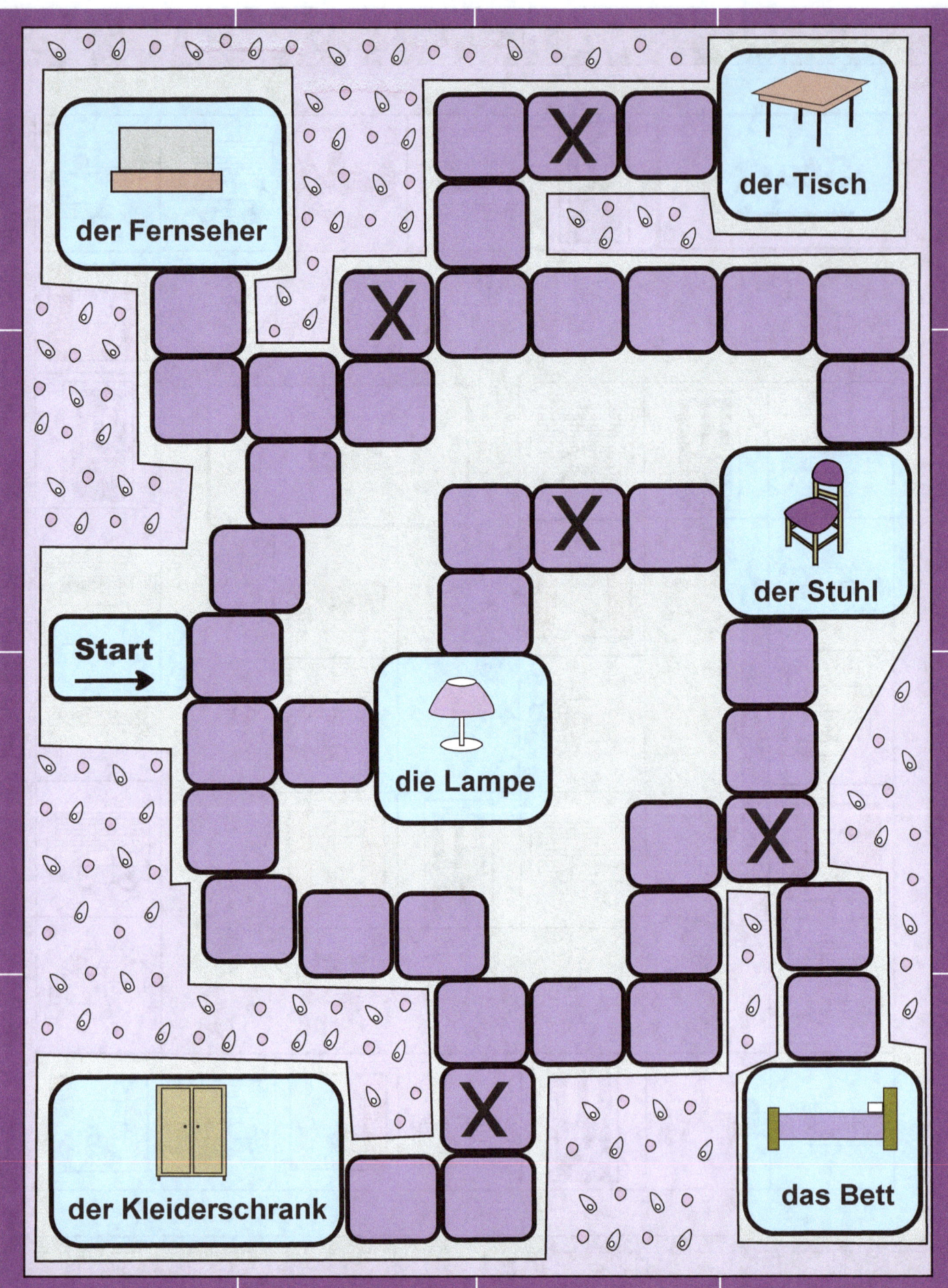

Die Möbel (the furniture)

Imagine you are buying some new furniture for your bedroom.
To win, you need to be the first person to get the following six items:

das Bett (the bed)

der Tisch (the table)

der Stuhl (the chair)

die Lampe (the lamp)

der Kleiderschrank (the wardrobe)

der Fernseher (the television)

To play:

Place your counter on Start. Roll the dice and move your counter that number of spaces. Count the number of spaces in German.

1	2	3	4	5	6
eins	zwei	drei	vier	fünf	sechs

If you arrive at a shop, say the German word for the item of furniture, and if you haven't got it yet, draw the item and write the word in German. Take turns to roll the dice.

If you arrive at a **X** you have to lose an item. You can choose which item you lose. Who will be the first to get all six items?

Der Nachtisch (the dessert)

For the snakes & ladders game you will need:
A **dice** (You can use a normal dice or make the dice on page 2.)
A **counter for each player** (You can use cubes, rubbers or make your own)

To play:

Place all the counters on **Start**.

The first player rolls the dice, and counts that number of spaces.

If there is a ladder in the final square, go up it.

If there is a snake in the final square, go down it.

Say in German what is in the final square you land on.

Take turns to roll the dice. To win, be the first to reach **Ziel**.

 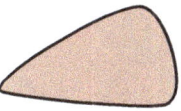 

der Kuchen (the cake) **der Apfelstrudel** (the apple pastry) **das Eis** (the ice cream)

der Joghurt (the yogurt) **der Obstsalat** (the fruit salad) **der Käse** (the cheese)

Das Obst (the fruit)

For the fruit game you will need:
A **dice** (You can use a normal dice or make the dice on page 2.)
A **counter for each player** (You can use cubes, rubbers or make your own)

To play:

Place all the counters on **Start**.

The first player rolls the dice, and counts that number of spaces.

Say in German what is in the final square you land on.

Take turns to roll the dice. To win, be the first to reach **Ziel**.

der Apfel
(the apple)

die Orange
(the orange)

die Banane
(the banana)

die Birne
(the pear)

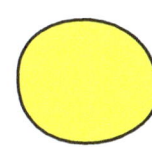
die Melone
(the melon)

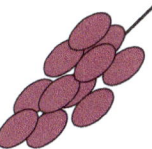
die Trauben
(the grapes)

Die Stadt (the town / city)

Imagine you are on holiday, and want to go to some places in the town where you are staying. To win, you need to be the first person to go to the following six places:

das Schwimmbad
(the swimming pool)

der Bahnhof
(the station)

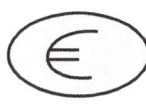

die Bank
(the bank)

das Schloss
(the castle)

das Museum
(the museum)

das Café
(the cafe)

To play:

Place your counter on Start. Roll the dice and move your counter that number of spaces. Count the number of spaces in German.

1	2	3	4	5	6
eins	zwei	drei	vier	fünf	sechs

If you arrive at a place in the town, say the German word for the place, and if you haven't been there yet, draw the place and write the word in German. Take turns to roll the dice.

If you arrive at a moon you have to miss a go.

Who will be the first to visit all six places?

Die Tiere (the animals)

For the snakes & ladders game you will need:
A **dice** (You can use a normal dice or make the dice on page 2.)
A **counter for each player** (You can use cubes, rubbers or make your own counters)

To play:

Place all the counters on **Start**.

The first player rolls the dice, and counts that number of spaces.

If there is a ladder in the final square, go up it.

If there is a snake in the final square, go down it.

Say in German what is in the final square you land on.

Take turns to roll the dice. To win, be the first to reach **Ziel**.

die Katze
(the cat)

die Schildkröte
(the tortoise)

der Hund
(the dog)

das Pferd
(the horse)

das Kaninchen
(the rabbit)

der Hamster
(the hamster)

Die Transportmittel (the transport)

For the transport board game you will need:
A **dice** (You can use a normal dice or make the dice on page 2.)
A **counter for each player** (You can use cubes, rubbers or make your own)

To play:

Place all the counters on **Start**.

Roll the dice, and count that number of spaces.

Say in German what is in the final square you land on.

Take turns to roll the dice. To win, be the first to reach **Ziel.**

das Auto
(a car)

das Flugzeug
(a plane)

der Bus
(a bus)

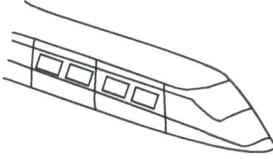

der Zug
(a train)

das Schiff
(a boat)

das Fahrrad
(a bike)

Das Wetter (the weather)

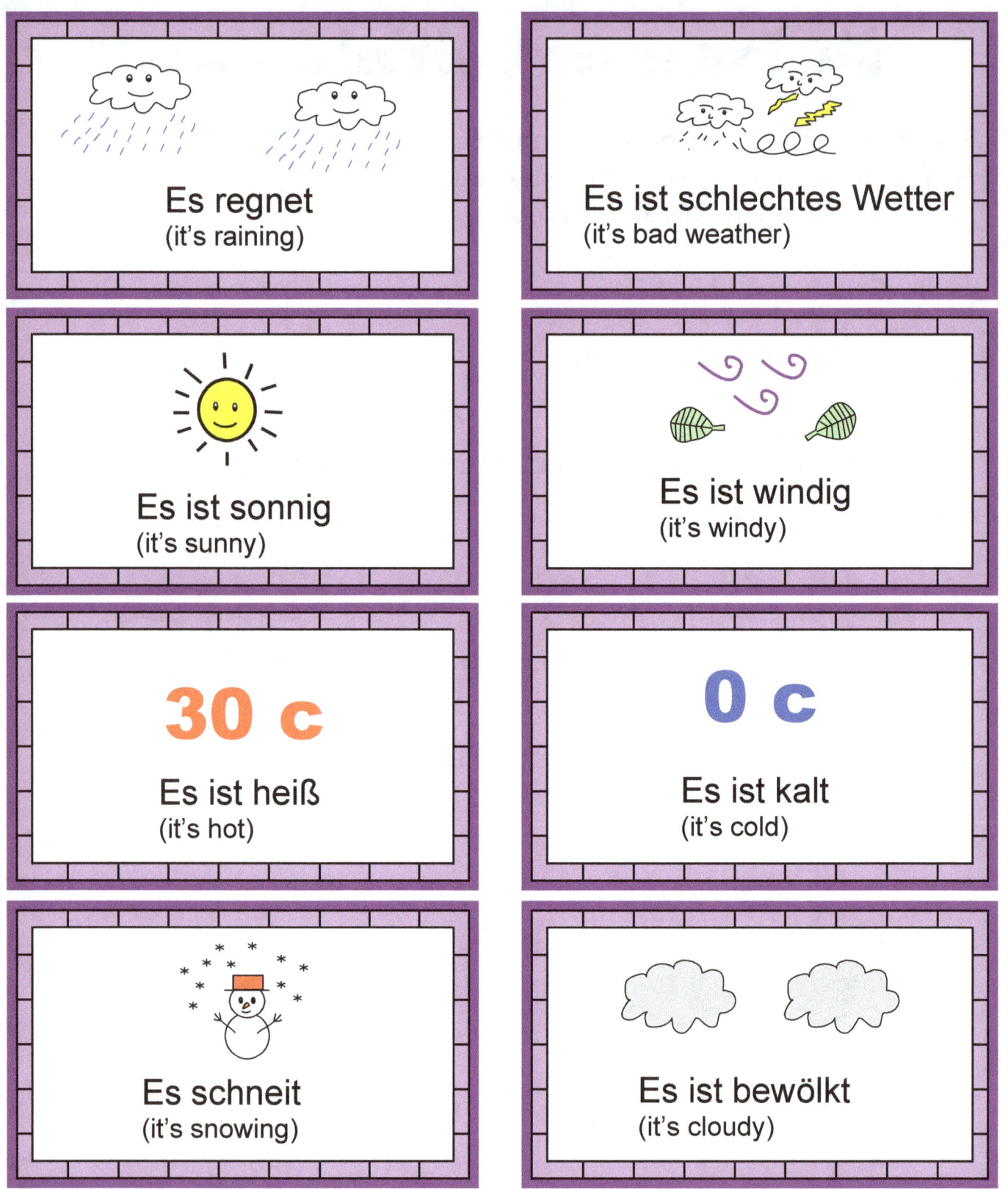

For the weather pairs game you will need to photocopy this page 2 or 4 times. Then, with an adult cut out the 8 cards per page. (Or make your own cards by copying the pictures and German words.)

To play: Place the cards face down. Take turns to choose two cards, saying the German weather phrase. Keep the cards that match and turn over the cards that don't. Who will win the most cards?

Der Zoo (the zoo)

Guess the German word

Each player chooses one of the German words from above. You can secretly write down your word if you want to. Take turns to guess the word of the other player or players. If you guess the word correctly, you win a point and everyone chooses a new word. To win, be the first to get 5 points.

Alternative game: Take turns to draw or do an action for one of the above. The other players have to guess the German word.

© Copyright Joanne Leyland 2021

The pages in this book may be photocopied for use at home or at school by the purchaser or purchasing institution only. They may not be reproduced electronically.

For children learning German there are also the following books by Joanne Leyland:

Cool Kids Speak German - Books 1, 2 and 3

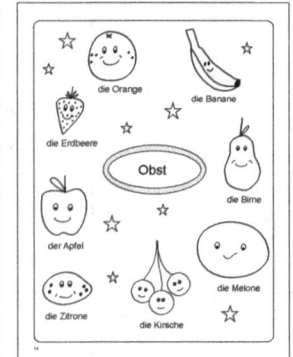 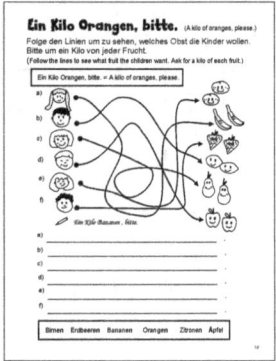 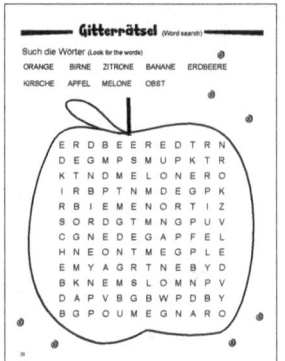

With 6 interesting topics in every book. Each topic starts with an introductory picture page showing all the words for that topic. These words are then practised, and sentences are built using the words. The topics end with a fun word search.

First 100 Words In German Coloring Book Cool Kids Speak German

The 100 German words include a dragon, a dinosaur, some food, transport, animals, toys and clothes. The 30 delightful pages all have borders and are single sided.

40 German Word Searches Cool Kids Speak German

The word searches appear in fun shapes and pictures accompany the German words so that each word search can be a meaningful learning activity. 40 Topics.

Photocopiable Games For Teaching German

Differentiated activities for children of various abilities. The games are colour coded according to the amount of German words in each game. The 8 great topics in this fantastic book include clothes, drinks, numbers, pet animals, fruit, food, sport and weather.

The games can be played to learn / revise German vocabulary or the pupils can practise making German sentences or questions as they play the games. For each topic there are ideas for making sentences or questions using the words in that topic, and you can choose what you want the pupils to practise as they play the games. Let's make learning German fun!

For more information about learning German and the great books by Joanne Leyland go to **https://fungermanforkids.com**

www.ingramcontent.com/pod-product-compliance
Lightning Source LLC
Chambersburg PA
CBHW081359080526
44588CB00016B/2551